My Emotions
Mes émotions

SAD
LA TRISTESSE

A Crabtree Roots Book

Un livre de la collection Les racines de Crabtree

AMY CULLIFORD

Crabtree Publishing
crabtreebooks.com

School-to-Home Support for Caregivers and Teachers

This book helps children grow by letting them practice reading. Here are a few guiding questions to help the reader with building his or her comprehension skills. Possible answers appear here in red.

Before Reading:

- What do I think this book is about?
    - *This book is about feeling sad.*
    - *This book is about what feeling sad looks like.*
- What do I want to learn about this topic?
    - *I want to learn what makes me feel sad.*
    - *I want to learn what feeling sad looks like.*

During Reading:

- I wonder why...
    - *I wonder why we frown when we are sad.*
    - *I wonder why we cry.*

What have I learned so far?

- *I have learned what feeling sad looks like.*
- *I have learned that people cry when they are sad.*

After Reading:

- What details did I learn about this topic?
    - *I have learned that there are many things that can make a person sad.*
    - *I have learned that it is good to tell people when you are sad so they can help.*
- Read the book again and look for the vocabulary words.
    - *I see the word **losing** on page 4 and the word **frown** on page 6. The other vocabulary words are found on page 14.*

Soutien de l'école à la maison pour les parents, les gardiens et les enseignants

Ce livre aide les enfants à se développer grâce à la pratique de la lecture. Voici quelques exemples de questions pour aider le lecteur ou la lectrice à développer ses capacités de compréhension. Les suggestions de réponses sont indiquées en rouge.

Avant la lecture

- De quoi ce livre parle-t-il?
    - *Ce livre parle du sentiment de la tristesse.*
    - *Ce livre explique à quoi ressemble la tristesse.*
- Qu'est-ce que je veux apprendre sur ce sujet?
    - *Je veux apprendre ce qui me rend triste.*
    - *Je veux apprendre à quoi ressemble le sentiment de la tristesse.*

Pendant la lecture

- Je me demande pourquoi...
    - *Je me demande pourquoi je fronce les sourcils quand je suis triste.*
    - *Je me demande pourquoi je pleure.*
- Qu'est-ce que j'ai appris jusqu'à présent?
    - *J'ai appris à quoi ressemble le sentiment de la tristesse.*
    - *J'ai appris que les gens pleurent quand ils sont tristes.*

Après la lecture

- Nomme quelques détails que tu as retenus.
    - *J'ai appris que plusieurs choses peuvent rendre une personne triste.*
    - *J'ai appris que je peux dire aux gens que je suis triste afin qu'ils puissent m'aider.*
- Lis le livre à nouveau et cherche les mots de vocabulaire.
    - *Je vois le mot **perdre** à la page 4 et le mot **fronce** à la page 6. Les autres mots de vocabulaire se trouvent à la page 14.*

What makes me **sad**?

Qu'est-ce qui me rend **triste**?

Losing makes me sad.

Perdre me rend triste.

I **frown** when I am sad.

Je **fronce** les sourcils quand je suis triste.

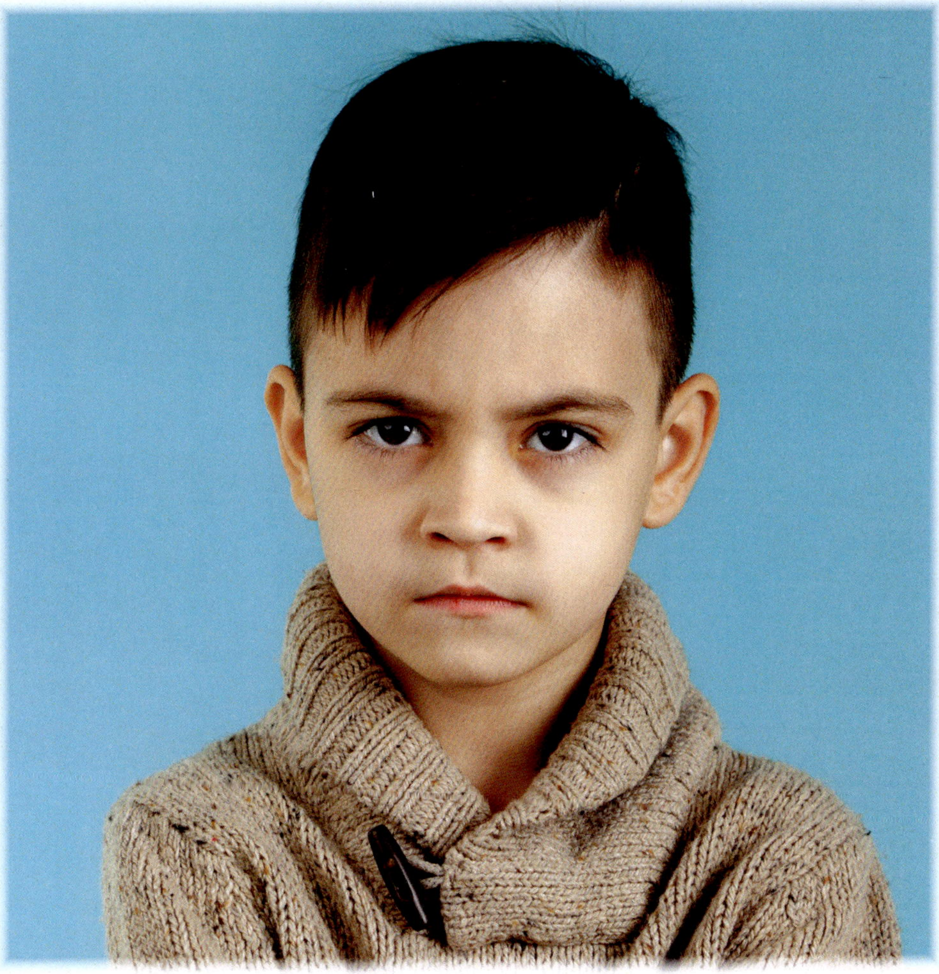

My **friend** moving away makes me sad.

Je suis triste quand mon **amie** déménage.

I **cry** when I am sad.

Je **pleure** quand je suis triste.

It is good to tell a friend if you are sad.

Tu peux dire à ton amie que tu es triste.

A friend can help you.

Ton amie peut t'aider.

What makes you sad?

Qu’est-ce qui te rend triste?

Word List / Liste de mots

Sight Words

a
am
good
I
makes
me
my
to
what
when
you

Mots courants

à
je
me
mon
quand
qu'est-ce
rend
suis
tu

Words to Know / La boîte à mots

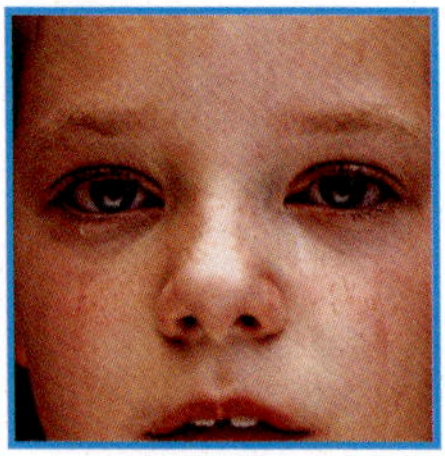

cry
pleure

friend
amie

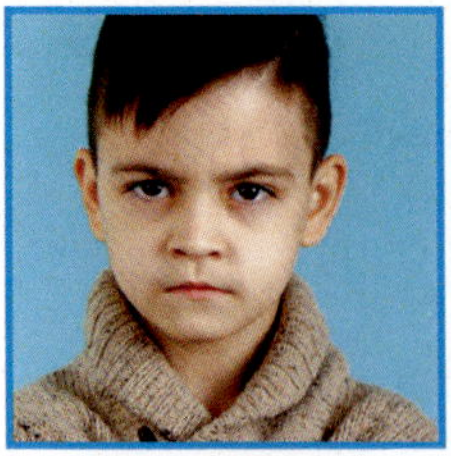

frown
fronce

losing
perdre

sad
triste

47 Words

What makes me **sad**?

Losing makes me sad.

I **frown** when I am sad.

My **friend** moving away makes me sad.

I **cry** when I am sad.

It is good to tell a friend if you are sad.

A friend can help you.

What makes you sad?

49 mots

Qu'est-ce qui me rend **triste**?

Perdre me rend triste.

Je **fronce** les sourcils quand je suis triste.

Je suis triste quand mon **amie** déménage.

Je **pleure** quand je suis triste.

Tu peux dire à ton amie que tu es triste.

Ton amie peut t'aider.

Qu'est-ce qui te rend triste?

My Emotions
SAD
Mes Émotions
LA TRISTESSE

Written by/Autrice: Amy Culliford
Designed by/Conception: Rhea Wallace
Series Development/Développement des séries: James Earley
Proofreader/Relectrice: Ellen Rodger
Educational Consultant/Conseillère pédagogique: Marie Lemke M.Ed.

Photographs/Photographhgies: Shutterstock: Juan Pablo Gonzaález: cover; Eveny Atamanenko: p. 1; icsnaps: p. 3, 14; Brocreative: p. 5, 14; Evgenyrychko: p. 7, 14; TTstock: p. 8, 14; Matryoha: p. 9, 14; szefei: p. 10-11; wavebreakmedia: p. 13

Crabtree Publishing

crabtreebooks.com 800-387-7650

Published in Canada
Publié au Canada
Crabtree Publishing
616 Welland Ave.
St. Catharines, Ontario
L2M 5V6

Published in the United Stat
Publié aux États-Unis
Crabtree Publishing
347 Fifth Avenue,
Suite 1402-145
New York, NY, 10016

Paperback 978-1-0398-5108-5
Ebook (pdf) 978-1-0398-5150-4
Epub 978-1-0398-5192-4

Printed in Canada/122023/CP20231116

Library and Archives Canada Cataloguing in Publication
Available at the Library and Archives Canada

Library of Congress Cataloging-in-Publication Data
Available at the Library of Congress